The Three Revolutionaries

By

Frank Hegyi

Partial financial support for the project.

Provided by the Cistel Foundation

Published by

Frank Hegyi Publications

Ottawa, Ontario, Canada

www.hegyipublication.com

© Frank Hegyi – 2016

ISBN 978-0-9940201-2-3

All rights reserved

Table of Contents

INTRODUCTION **5**

MY ANCESTORS **7**

   Mihály Hegyi in the 1848 Revolutions 7

   My Grandfather 17

   István Hegyi' escape to Yougslavia 27

   My role in the Hungarian Revolution, beginning in 1956 . 33

RE-BUILDING MY LIFE **51**

PUBLICATIONS AND SOCIAL WORK **59**

   My Social Life 69

   Joining the Private Sector 79

TRADITIONAL PUBLICATIONS OF BOOKS **97**

SELF-PUBLISHING OF BOOKS **109**

   Lightning Source by Ingram 109

   My web site 113

   Journey to the Big World 115

   The Stroke 117

   Death Can Wait 121

   If It Wasn't for Celibacy... I Would Have Been a Priest .. 125

SOCIAL MEDIA PROMOTIONS **127**

   Facebook 129

The Book Promoters 131

EPILOGUE 133

LITERATURE CITED 137

Introduction

This book is about three revolutionist: my great-great grand Father, my Uncle István and I.

My great-great grandfather, a Hungarian nobleman, visited the Hapsburg Castle on many occasions. The Estate in western Hungary and it was about 150 kilometers to the north-west to Vienna. He joined the 1848 revolution and was killed as a member of the Hungarian patriarchy. His estate was confiscated and my great grandfather was brought up as a citizen in Szemegye, Vas megye. My grandfather tried to rebuild the family fortune and succeeded to a certain aspect but my father lost it in 1952 as part of the collectivisation. I grew up while my father fought the government and we became very poor. So, in 1956 I joined the revolution against the Soviet occupation. Our insurrection was defeated in November 4, 1956 and I escaped only 3 hours before youth leaders, including myself, were to be executed.

The following book covers the stories of my family's part in the revolutions. My great-great grandfather died as part of the patriarchy. My Uncle spent 5 years in a death camp, and I escaped to the west and rebuilt my life as a scientist, government employee and an entrepreneur.

My Ancestors

Mihály Hegyi in the 1848 Revolutions

My great-great grandfather was an inspiration to me: his political views, devotion to his home land, and his final sacrifice was the guiding principle in my life

My great-great grandfather, Mihály Hegyi, born in 1820, was a very active nobleman, of the Hegyi de Pápa. He travelled to Vienna many times to represent his estate within the Habsburg Empire and was a follower of the teachings of Count István Szécheni. Many referred to Szécheni as the 'Greatest Hungarian', in promoting the Hungarian language and the development of the Hungarian Academy of Sciences. But, he was not convinced that the Habsburg Empire was the most beneficial political system during that time. Hegyi was also a student of the poet Sándor Petőfi; especially inspired by "On Your Feet Hungarian" a national poem of the 1848 Revolutions[1]:

Rise up, Magyar, the country calls!
It's 'now or never' what fate befalls...
Shall we live as slaves or free men?
That's the question - choose your `Amen'

God of Hungarians, we swear unto Thee,

We swear unto Thee –

That slaves we shall no longer be!

---

[1]

https://images.search.yahoo.com/yhs/search;_ylt=AwrTca8Cq4NXiYsAgucPxQt.;_ylu=X3oDMTByNWU4cGh1BGNvbG8DZ3ExBHBvcwMxBHZ0aWQDBHNlYwNzYw--?p=S%C3%A1ndor+Pet%C5%91fi&fr=yhs-adk-adk_sbnt&hspart=adk&hsimp=yhs-adk_sbnt#id=17&iurl=http%3A%2F%2Ffenymag.hu%2Ffile%2F2015%2F07%2FPet%C5%91fi-S%C3%A1ndor.jpg&action=click

Sándor Petőfi. The Hungarian Poet

On the 17 March 1848, Batthyány created the first Hungarian Diet or House of Parliament. Responsible government was formed, with Ministers Lajos Batthyány (prime minister), Lajos Kossuth (finance minister), Ferenc Deák (minister of justice), István Széchenyi (minister of labour, infrastructure and transport), and Pál Antal Esterházy (Minister besides the King (roughly Foreign Minister).

The Thee Revolutionaries

Count Lajos Batthyány, Hungarian landowner, politician and the first prime minister in 1848

After a simultaneous Austrian revolution in Vienna was defeated, the **kamarilla** orchestrated the replacement of **Ferdinand I by his nephew Franz Joseph I of Austria**. The new young monarch Franz Joseph I (18 years old) didn't recognise Batthyány's premiere or revision of laws. In the end, the final break between Vienna and Pest occurred when Field-Marshal **Count Franz Philipp von Lamberg** was given control of every army in Hungary (including Jelačić's). Lamberg went to Hungary where he was mobbed and murdered.

Following his death, the Imperial court dissolved the Hungarian Diet and appointed Jelačić (a Croatian land load) as Regent. Meanwhile, Batthyány travelled again to Vienna to seek a compromise with the new Emperor. His efforts remained unsuccessful as Francis Joseph I refused to accept the reform laws (Batthyány laws). On 13 September 1848 Batthyány announced a rebellion and requested that the Palatine (Hungarian governor) lead them. However the Palatine, under the Emperor's orders, resigned and left Hungary. This was a great setback for the Hungarian Prime Minister.

Hungary now had war raging on three fronts: Jelačić's Croatian troops to the south, Romanians in Banat and in Transylvania to the East, and Austria to the West. The lack of soldiers created a serious military crisis for the Hungarian government. They sent Kossuth (a brilliant orator) to recruit volunteers for the new Hungarian army. While Croatian ban Josip Jelačić was marching on Pest, Kossuth went from town to town rousing the people to the defense of the country, and the popular force of the Honvéd (or the Hungarian national army) was his creation. My great-great grandfather joined the revolution in the division of Huszars (the horse cavalry). With the help of Kossuth's recruiting speech, Batthyány was successful in his hurried effort to organize the Hungarian Revolutionary Army. The new army defeated the Croatians on 29 of September at the Battle of Pákozd. The battle became an icon for the Hungarian army because of its influence on politics and positive morale.

Mihály Hegyi fought in the battle of Pákozd as an officer of the army and contributed greatly to the Hungarian victory. His heart's desire was to defend Hungary against all odds, especially against Jelačić's Croatian army (the Emperors' army). The Hungarian army was victorious and Jelačić withdrew his troops.

Later Batthyány came to an impasse with the Emperor, especially the view that Field-Marshal Count Franz Philipp von Lamberg died in Hungary, murdered by Hungarian rebels. So on 2 October he resigned as prime minister and his seat in parliament. When Batthyány resigned, he appointed Szemere (another

Hungarian noble man) to carry on the government provisionally. At the end of September Szemere was made President of the Committee of National Defense and Kossuth was elected as the Hungarian head of state.

The new Szemere government was formed on 2 of May, 1849. Kossuth played a key role in tying down the Hungarian army for weeks in the siege and recapture of Buda castle succeeding on 4 May 1849. The hopes of ultimate success were, however, frustrated by the intervention of Russia when the tsar sent 200,000 troops to the aid of the Habsburg Empire. Kossuth reached out to the western powers but in vain, and on the 11 of August, Kossuth abdicated. He was replaced by Görgey who capitulated at Világos (now Şiria, Romania) on August 13, 1849 to the Russians, and handed over the army to the Austrians. The Emperor sought revenge and executed Batthyány and 13 top ranking military officers on October 6, 1849.

The Thee Revolutionaries

Batthyány's execution on October 6, 1849

The Thee Revolutionaries

In Arad, 13 Hungarian Officers (12 Generals and one Colonel) were also executed the same day.

My great-great grandfather died in the Battle of Vilagos. He was buried in a mass grave along with Petőfi and hundreds of soldiers. The Emperor Franz Joseph I also imprisoned many other members of the Hungarian military.

My great grandmother and her son (4 years old), fearing execution from the Hapsburg Empire, escaped the family home servants' help and settled in the village of Szemegye, Vas megye. The estate was confiscated by the Hapsburg Empire and my great grandfather grew up as a farm labourer in Szemegye.

My Grandfather

I had a special relationship with Grandfather. He was my hero in all aspects

My grandfather, born in 1870, finished Grade 4 in school before working as a farm labourer. By the time he was 20 years old, he became an entrepreneur by bidding on jobs in neighbouring estates. He supplied labourers for hoeing potato and corn fields, harvesting crops such as wheat, rye and barley, and picking apples and plums in fruit orchards. At age 24 he went to a dance in Szemegye and asked a beautiful young girl, Anna Vajkovics, for a csardas (a fast Hungarian folk dance). He was a tall (over 6 feet) handsome man with a typical bushy moustache and wore black riding boots which were fashionable at the time. Anna complimented his dancing which encouraged him to ask for the next dance...again and again, until they played the last slow waltz. He asked permission to accompany Anna to the front gate of her home to find out where she lived.

The next Sunday afternoon, my grandfather, still wearing his Sunday best suit, reserved mainly for church, walked to Anna's house. (Picture at the front of the book, my grandfather on the left). According to Grandfather, Anna was hoping that he would call on her because she was still in her church dress at 3 in the afternoon! The Sunday visits became regular and two years later, Grandfather asked Anna's father for her hand in marriage. Since Grandfather's business was expanding to nearby villages, and Anna's parents were getting on in age, the two of them decided to live in the Vajkovics' home in Szemegye.

Grandfather always talked affectionately about Grandmother, what a beautiful smile she had, how well she danced. They both shared an entrepreneurial spirit and the dream of buying land they could call their own and a large family. Grandmother was an excellent cook and according to Grandfather, she made the best pork schnitzel and pork goulash with nokedli (spaetzel) that he ever tasted. One evening, when Grandfather paid his many compliments for the good meal, Grandmother suggested that they could earn extra money by feeding the contract farm workers, many of whom were single men and would welcome a good home cooked meal. Initially, they started feeding just a few laborers who worked on nearby farms, but the business expanded as fast as the reputation of my grandmother's cooking spread to other workers. Since Grandmother always made sure that everyone had a good meal, she usually cooked a little bit more than the men could eat. Grandfather then had the idea of raising pigs on the leftover food. This venture became highly profitable as they had to buy less pork to feed the men. In less than 10 years they saved up enough to buy a farm of their own. Grandmother had a brother in Nyögér so they took a horse drawn carriage to make a visit to this upland village and look for land to purchase. Luck was on their side as a 34-hectare and highly fertile lot was up for sale after the death of the owner. The land came with a nice house on the main street with a large backyard, a stable for 10 animals and a barn. They had enough savings to pay for this farm in cash and, according to Grandfather they even had money left over to buy another horse and 4 dairy cows. So, in 1906 my grandparents moved to

Nyőgér. They already had an 8 year old daughter, Maria, a 6 year old son, Antal, and a 2 year old son, Ferenc (my father). In 1908 they had a daughter, Margit, and another girl, Emi, was born in 1910. The youngest of the Hegyi children was born in 1914, a boy named István.

My grandfathers' family

My grandfather turned out to be a successful farmer and the land produced enough food and other goods for the family to have a comfortable living and even allowed the children to have an education past the traditional 4th grade. Maria completed grade 6 and Antal went beyond grade school to graduate from a 2-year forest technician course. My father was enrolled in a seminary to be a priest (with strong persuasion from grandmother) after finishing grade 6 but lasted only 2 months. He escaped through a second story window and went home to tell his father that he wanted to be a farmer just like him. Margit and Emi both finished grade 6 and István was considered to be the brain, because he managed to graduate from Gimnázium, a 4-year high school, after which he got a well-paying job in an office.

My grandfather was a well-respected leader in the village of Nyőgér. He served as a legal advisor in the village and had a statue built in the church yard to commemorate his achievements.

My grandfather had tears in his eyes each time he talked about the tragic day of June 1st, 1933 when my grandmother died of an illness which appeared to be a bad case of influenza. He never married again. Nobody could ever take the place of his true love, my grandmother. The eldest daughter, Maria, stepped in to run the house after the death of Grandmother, but she left the Hegyi home 2 years later to marry a "well to do" farmer in the neighboring village of Sótóny. After Maria left the house, my Grandfather took up all the chores.

My father had gradually taken over from Grandfather, running the farm. As tradition would suggest, he began to look for a wife to help him with the chores. In 1935 he went to a dance in Püspökmolnári, a village about 20 km from Nyögér. There, he met a petite young girl, Sarolta Piri. She was home for the weekend from the Eszterházi Castle near Sopron, where she worked as an assistant chef. After a 2 year courtship, the 33 year old Ferenc married the 24 year old Sarolta. On June 9, 1938 I was born on the kitchen table, delivered by a midwife.

After World War II, Hungary faced the challenge of choosing a new government. In November of 1945, general elections were held and the Smallholder Party won 57 percent of the vote, with the communists winning only 17 percent, even with Moscow's domination or interference in the election. The Soviet commander in Hungary, Marshal Voroshilov, refused to allow the Smallholders to form a government. Instead Voroshilov established a coalition government with the Smallholders and Communists, with the communists holding all key posts. Rajk became minister of the interior and in this post established the security police. In February of 1947, the police began arresting leaders of the Smallholder Party and the National Peasant Party. Several prominent figures in both parties escaped abroad. Dr. Zoltan Tildy was named President, and Dr. Ferenc Nagy, Prime Minister. Mátyás Rákosi, (a communist) was named the Deputy Prime Minister. The Red Army still occupied Hungary, and the communists wanted complete control of the government. They created the AVO (Allamvedélmi Osztály), which served as the communists' secret police and Gábor Péter was named as director. Péter began a series of Stalinesque purges to cut away the foundation of the Smallholder party. The AVO arrested the most outspoken critics of the communists, accusing them of Fascist coercion. In May of 1947, Prime Minister Nagy went on Holiday in Switzerland. He was told that if he returned, he would be arrested. In August of that same year, the communists won 24 percent of the popular vote in the general elections. The Hungarian Communist Party became the largest single party in the elections of 1947 and served in the coalition People's Independence Front government. The communists gradually gained control of the government and, by 1948, the Social Democratic Party ceased to exist as an independent organization.

In January 1948 Rákosi, now the President, reduced the government to a one party coalition. Soon after that, Rákosi was called to Moscow. There, he was told László Rajk, the minister of the Interior, and Péter's boss had been identified as working with Marshall Tito, the Yugoslavian dictator and an Anti-Stalinist.

Mátyás Rákosi, President of the party

When Rákosi returned to Budapest, he held a cabinet meeting (minus Rajk). It was decided that Rajk had to go. On May 30, Rajk was arrested and charged with treason. He was then beaten and tortured by the AVO, in what would be a vain attempt at a forced confession. The beatings continued until at least June 11th when it was realized that Rajk would not give in. Péter threatened Rajk's family, and told him that the entire affair was a put-up job or a false promise, that his family would be spared, and relocated in the Soviet Union under a new identity. In the end, Rajk confessed to his crimes. His last words before execution were "Long live Communism". Altogether, 15 people were executed and 78 were imprisoned[2] that day/month/year.

Laszlo Rajk, Minister of Interior.

[2] https://en.wikipedia.org/wiki/L%C3%A1szl%C3%B3_Rajk

István Hegyi' escape to Yougslavia

Uncle István was a true patriot, but he paid a price for his devotion to the homeland. He spent 5 years in jail after his escape to Yugoslavia.

István Hegyi was my father's younger brother (born in 1914), the first to finish high school, and the intellectual of the family. In 1948 he attempted to immigrate to Yugoslavia. My family thought it was Prime Minister Tito's interest in independence from the Soviet Union. But, the border guard, loyal to Moscow, handed him back to Hungary. Then his persecution began. First, he was taken to Szombathely and tortured extensively before being transported to the AHO headquarters in Budapest where he was subjected to further torture. He spent nights bare-footed in a cell that had water running through it and rats swimming around. The cruelty included beatings with rubber batons until he became unconscious (a special treatment designed by Rákosi). Two or three policemen would kick him with boots when he fell to the floor, until he passed out He was stood naked in a small cell and if he leaned on a wall, would receive a painful electric shock. They pushed salt into his mouth and he was forced to drink water from the toilet bowl. He went without food for days, without sleep for many nights and was handcuffed and in leg irons for many days and nights.

Fellow prisoners included former communist leaders (of non-Moscow origin), intellectuals, writers, farmers, labourers and priests. The guards used to brag about the treatment that was especially designed by Rákosi for priests. After several beatings, a priest would be given a crucifix to kiss. But the crucifix was charged with electricity and sometimes the dose was large enough to electrocute the priest. Prime Minister Rákosi had trained in the Soviet Union on torture, and copied Stalin extensively.

The torture was designed to get a false confession that my uncle was an agent of the foreign imperialists under Tito's control. Since my uncle was identified with Tito, he was tortured extensively toward this aim. When he could not take the pain anymore, he signed a confession that he could not even read because his eyes were too swollen from the beatings. He was then taken to the labour camp at Recsk, also called a death camp. There, the purpose was to torture prisoners on a continuous basis. He said the first day he was taken outside to work in below freezing temperatures. When he tripped and fell into the snow in front of one of the guards, the guard stepped on his bare hands with his spiked boots. The guard twisted his leg until blood was pouring out of my uncle's hand. He had to tear off a piece from his shirt to bandage the hand so that he could continue working without gloves.

Uncle István told us how determined he was in surviving, even though the AVO guards kept telling him that it was a death camp, that he was there to suffer and die as soon as he was too weak to work. He managed to keep up his strength. Besides working in the quarry, he did push ups and other exercises. When he came home he did not fit into the riding boots that he was wearing before his internment because of his increased leg muscles.

Imre Nagy, Prime Minister.

When Imre Nagy came come to power in 1953, István was freed. He was never the same man as the torture had reduced him, both physically and mentally. My family is always grateful to Nagy for the release of my uncle. István continued his writing, by hand, of the stories of the Soviet occupation and life in general. My aunts have always admired his writing, although he never published an article.

This picture was taken in 1979 with his son beside him (to his right).

My Uncle (white haired), his son with my Mother and Father.

My role in the Hungarian Revolution, beginning in 1956.

I joined the revolution in 1956 to fight the aggression of communism. After the revolution was defeated, I escaped to Austria

I was born in June 1938 on the kitchen table and delivered by a midwife. By the time I was 3 years old, I was greatly influenced by the many stories my grandfather told me about the world. After being scolded by my mother, I decided to leave home. I asked my mother to pack me a lunch and I left. The village Priest (Dr. Lenarsics) saw me leaving my home, took this picture of me (Picture in the front of the book, right side). He asked me where I was going and I replied 'into the big world.' My mother, who was watching from the window, came out to escort me back. That was my first adventure on leaving home.

I was 3 years old when I first ventured out to see the world.

After the Second World War finished in 1945, the communist takeover of Hungary occurred. My father inherited the farm from my grandfather. He was a proud man and the farm produced enough goods for the winter.

My mother and I in 1950

A lady from the local office (Eva) was determined to get my father into the collective farm. In 1955, with the best harvest, she taxed my father enough that he was forced to give up the farm. During the winter of 1955, my mother and I collected acorns to feed the pigs on the collective farm and with the proceeds we were able to buy bread and other goods. My father was a labourer in the collective farm, looking after cows.

I finished high school (grade 8) in 1954 and worked as a labourer for a year to support the family. My Uncle István was in prison and I was not allowed to continue my education for political reasons. However, my goal was to get into high school. My father was not convinced about my goal to further my education, but my mother was receptive to my plans. In the fall of 1955, I was allowed into high school after my uncle was freed from prison. I was a good student, getting nigh marks, and in the final year, was enrolled into University of Pécs to study Law.

In October 1956 I was attending high school in Sárvár. I had just started my 4th year in the Gimnázium. On October 24th I got up at 6 am at the place where my mother arranged room and board for me during the school year. I turned on the radio and started to shave. First I thought that the reception was bad on the radio because I was hearing loud cracking noises. Then the announcer said, with a highly excited voice: "Dear listeners, you are hearing the sound of machine guns. Yesterday, university students were peacefully demonstrating on the streets, and the AVH (AVO, the Hungarian secret police), fired on them, killing many students, women and children. As a result, the fighting has now spread throughout Budapest. Hungary has erupted into a revolution.

I got dressed and rode my bicycle to the high school at 8 am. There were many students outside the building, talking about the revolution. One of our teachers came out and told us to go home and wait until we were called back to school through the radio.

I rode my bicycle back to my place and told the landlady what was happening in Budapest. Mrs. Pasti was in her 60's, a widow without any children, so she treated me like a grandson. We agreed that I might as well go home to my parents until things settled. I packed my books and clothes, strapped the suitcase on the back of the bicycle and started my 10 km trip to the village of Nyögér where my parents lived. When I got home around noon, my parents were very excited that a revolution was in full swing in Budapest and the hope of soon gaining our freedom from the Soviet occupation. I spent the afternoon visiting friends and speculating on what was going on in Budapest. We did not have television and radio was the only medium for news. Street names where the fighting was occurring did not mean much to us. We noted that the students who were throwing Molotov cocktails on Russian tanks were about the same age or just a couple of years older than I was. My father commented that if I was allowed to go to high school when I finished grade 8, I would be at a University and very likely in the middle of the fighting.

That evening at 6 pm there was a mass in our Roman Catholic parish church. The priest, Father Imre Lenarsics, was well known for his anti-communist views. He delivered a compassionate message to the faithful to support the revolution. Our church was the parish for two other villages as well. There was only standing room as people looked for direction from the priest. Even during communist control, everyone respected or feared the priest because he made it clear that we needed him to give us absolution before we could go to heaven.

At the end of the mass, as people were coming out of church, Father Lenarsics at the main door suggested that somebody recite the patriotic poem of Petőfi, an inspiration to the 1848 freedom fight against the Austrians. Since I was standing near the priest, several people volunteered me to do the honour. I was well known in the village for my theatrical activities, a leading actor in a touring troupe, and often recited poetry on special occasions. I did not have to be asked twice. Petőfi was my favourite poet and I knew the requested poem, "Talpra Magyar" (Rise up Magyar) by heart. I stood on the top of the stairs leading to the main entrance of the church, while the parishioners gathered around. I was about 10 stairs above the ground so I could see the faces of the people waiting. I took my cap off, paused for a moment, and then started:

"On your feet Hungarians"... Even my father recited the verse:

God of Hungarians, we swear unto Thee,

We swear unto Thee - that slaves we shall

No longer be!

I recited four verses and the crowd joined me with the refrain at the end of each verse. As I recited the refrain, I put my left hand on my heart and raised the right hand in a victory sign. The crowd followed me with this gesture and I could see elderly farmers with tears coming from their eyes. When I reached the end of the poem, the crowd gave me enthusiastic applause that I never experienced on stage before.

My performance inspired people and encouraged the establishment of a Revolutionary Youth Council. Since reciting the poem earned me status in the village, I was nominated and acclaimed as Chairman of the Council. I accepted this honour and responsibility because I believed that communism had to be defeated by the people who were exploited by the cruel regime.

When I went to bed that night I couldn't sleep at all. So many thoughts were running through my head. I had just been elected as a student leader and we would call ourselves Freedom Fighters. In Budapest, University students were risking their lives in the fight for freedom. As the revolution continued, we heard on the radio that several army units joined in the fight against the Soviet occupiers. One person came home from Budapest and told us that students were making Molotov cocktails and throwing them from the tops of buildings into open trucks carrying Russian soldiers.

I was faced with a difficult decision that evening. Even though I had recited the patriotic poem of Petőfi, I could still pull back and watch the events unfolding. I could tell people in the morning that I didn't want to be chairman of the Revolutionary Youth Council. But then I thought how each time I was shaving, I would have to look in the mirror and see a person who didn't have the guts to fight for what he believed in and for his beloved country. My great-great grandfather had the willingness to fight in the 1848 revolution, for which he paid the ultimate price, his life. But he brought honour to the Hegyi name. My grandfather had instilled in me the importance of fighting for what one believes in.

The next morning when I got up and started to shave, I knew what I had to do in order to be proud of the face in front of me. Our Youth Council met around 10 am on October 26th. Angry villagers rounded up some of the local communists and were ready to punish them. They were demanding to hang Eva, the tax collector who was accountable for the heavy fines on people in order to force them into the collective farm. She was the one responsible for our family going without food during the winter of 1952. Farmers, including my father, were chanting "hang the bitch". Antal Bácsi who gave me a job in the summers was among them and now I had the task of chairing his trial by the Revolutionary Tribunal. This Tribunal has the responsibility to oversee the transition from communism to the private sector. Many of the villagers were after blood. I felt that if we killed Eva, we would be as bad as the AVH guards who had tortured my uncle István. I managed to convince the group that the real enemies were the Soviet occupiers. I suggested that we focus on helping the freedom fighters in Budapest and let the legal system deal with the local communist leaders in due course. I was supported in this stand by the Youth Council and the communist leaders were put under house arrest as the village had no jail.

I spent the next week organizing the shipment of food to Budapest to support the freedom fighters. Farmers brought flour, smoked meat, potatoes and canned fruit to the storage room of the collective farm. Antal Bácsi had the keys for the storage room. He helped us collect the food and even arranged with the truck driver of the collective farm to take the supplies to

Budapest, a 4-hour drive. Privately he thanked me for my calm during the trial. He was a man of high integrity, believed strongly in the principles of communism, but he was not a supporter of the cruel Stalin-Rákosi regime. Although he was secretary of the local communist party, he never hurt anyone, even during the most repressive period of the Rákosi rule.

There was jubilation in the village when Imre Nagy began to negotiate the withdrawal of Soviet troops from October 24 to November 4th. . Villagers were dancing on the street when we heard that Imre Nagy's government has also disbanded the AVH, promised free elections, and gave notice to withdraw from the Warsaw Pact.

The most important aspect of the political changes for the village was the possibility of having enough food and money for clothing. While the cessation of the AVH terror was welcome news, villagers had adjusted to the lifestyle. You couldn't trust your neighbors, friends or even your family members when it came to AVH internment. So people stopped talking about politics and the regime. However, it was more difficult to accept the fact that the farmers worked hard but the regime would take most of the produce away, leaving insufficient amounts for their use. Now, people were very hopeful that Imre Nagy was on their side. He had a good knowledge of agriculture and a reputation of fairness towards farmers.

On November 4, 1956, the red army launched a major attack on Hungary, aimed at crushing the spontaneous national uprising that had begun 12 days earlier. At 5:20 a.m., Hungarian Prime Minister Imre Nagy announced the invasion of the nation in a grim, 35-second broadcast, declaring: "Our troops are fighting. The Government is in its place." However, within hours, Nagy himself would seek asylum at the Yugoslav Embassy in Budapest. His former colleague, János Kádár, had been flown secretly from Moscow to the city of Szolnok, 60 miles southeast of the capital, and took power with Moscow's backing.

As former Chairman of the Youth Revolutionary Council, (went into hiding on November 4th) I found myself facing the possibility of going to jail or even being shot. The news spread quickly that the police had started to round up students who were youth leaders in the revolution. Some of them were shot on the spot, while others were imprisoned. I went into hiding in the village, sleeping in barns and haystacks, changing my location frequently.

On Sunday evening, November 18th my grandfather brought food to my hiding place and told me of the conversation he overheard in the smoke shop. A police captain, Pallosi, originally from the village but now a senior police officer in a nearby town, was looking for me. Pallosi was telling people that he was looking for that Hegyi kid. The next day, at noon on the steps of the church, he would be shot like the rest of the teenage terrorists.

For the last time, I gave my grandfather a big hug, and asked him what I should do. Should I come out of hiding or try to make it to Austria? Grandfather looked at me with tearful eyes and said: "Remember what they did to your uncle, István. I don't want that to happen to you. I love you, Grandson." We stood and Grandfather stared at me with a far-away look in his eyes and said: "Go to the big world, live our dream." We both agreed that we shouldn't tell my parents about this plan because they would be too emotional to understand the danger that I was in. We talked about how I could send a message back from Austria (if I made it) to let them know that I was safe without putting the family in harm's way with the police. We agreed on a coded message through Radio Free Europe: "Golden Lamb has arrived safely." My grandfather said that he would be glued to the radio and when he heard the message, he would talk to my parents. Knowing that this was the last time that I would see my grandfather was a deeply emotional moment for me. The tears blurred my vision as I watched his tall figure disappear in the darkness.

After I said goodbye to Grandfather, our Youth Revolutionary Council met for the last time. My cousin Imre who came home from Budapest, attended the meeting and told us that he was involved in throwing Molotov cocktails from the top of the buildings into armored Soviet vehicles. He said that he was definitely going to try to escape to Austria because he would be executed for his activities during the revolution. He thought that our council members were not in danger. But the youth leaders had been declared terrorists and many of them were already shot. This news, combined with the conversation my grandfather overheard, left no doubt in my mind that if I was captured, the probability of being shot the next day was very high. Imre suggested that we try to escape together early the next morning. I agreed and we started to develop a strategy for the escape. Two of our friends offered to take two bicycles out of the village at night and hide them at a location about 1 km west of the village.

We escaped from the hiding place in the village at 9 am the next day. We rode our bicycles on the back roads to Püspökmolnári where my mother's father lived. We said our goodbyes to the relatives and started out on foot to the border, about 35 kilometres from my grandparents' house. We went from wooded area to wooded area, hiding from the police. We had to cross a road and when we were on it, a group of Russian soldiers came by and surrounded us with machine guns. I was speaking Russian and told them: "Hello comrades, we are going home to our village." I reached into my pockets and got them the Komsomol ID (the young communist papers). As a high school student, we were all members of the Komsomol movement. When the leader examined my identification, the machine guns were lowered and cigarettes were offered and they wished us a good trip. The armoured car was travelling to the border and when it is disappeared, we took to the field of barley and travelled in it.

When we reached the border it was around 11 pm and our group had grown to about 200 people. When one man said that the border could be mined, we looked for volunteers to go across. I volunteered because at the time I did not fear death. I just wanted to get across, or blow up, whichever came first. I crawled out on my stomach and with each movement, visualized that my life would end. It was the most agonizing 10 minutes of my life and when I got across the border, the two hundred refugees followed in my track. The Austrian border guards escorted us to a refugee camp; we were safe again.

I sent a message to my Grandfather that we were in Austria: "Golden lamb has arrived safely". Then I participated in a number of interviews geared to establish me as a refugee and to place me in a country who welcomed us.

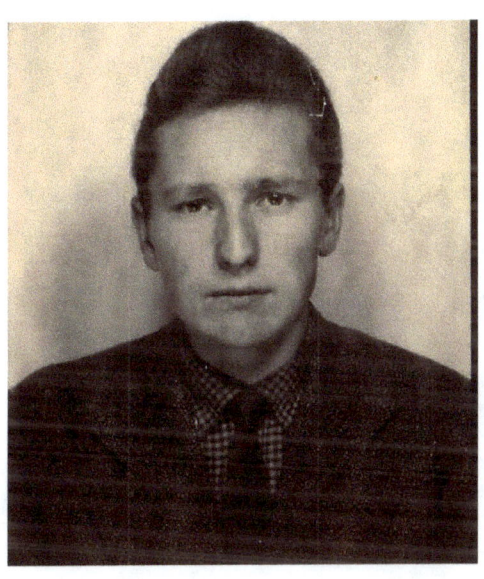

My refugee picture in Austria.

The Thee Revolutionaries

Re-building My Life

The first Christmas I cried for my homeland. Then the true Hegyi spirit guided me to rebuild my life

We spent 2 weeks in an Austrian refugee camp before taking a train from Graz to Salzburg. The next day, we flew to London, England. We were interns there in another refugee camp for 2 weeks. After a series of interviews, 12 of us (including my cousin) were transported by bus into Halifax, Yorkshire. We were housed in a Salvation Army hostel for 3 weeks, and an interpreter (Mrs. Dillinger) rented a cottage near Hebden Bridge, where we brought in our first Christmas away from home. On Christmas Eve I went outside and had a good cry. I was only 18, away from home in a strange land, could not speak the language and felt so lonely. Then, my thoughts turned to the future. I was going to succeed! The second Hegyi in our family had a reputation to succeed, and it was my turn. I was in a free country, I would work hard, and find success.

After Christmas, three of us got jobs in an Austin Brother factory pressing trousers.

In 1957 in am in Halifax, Yorkshire with Mrs Dillinger on my lap.

I worked hard studying English and joined a Roman Catholic Church in Halifax. After a mass I met a nice family and Mr. Gillespie invited me to play a game of snooker. Then, the next Sunday, after mass, they invited me to their place for lunch. Mr. and Mrs. Gillespie had two daughters (older then myself) and the Sunday outing included me after church. I confided in Mrs. Gillespie that I would like to continue my studies. My English is getting better and I would like to go to finish the High School studies. She helped me to get in touch with a high school principal and we were invited to a meeting. I was to ask the principal how I could graduate by taking courses in the evening. He wanted to see my level of studies and he presented me with a series of high school examples in mathematics. I solved the one in calculus.

Mr. and Mrs. Gillespie with their Daughter at Maureen's Wedding.

Then about a month later, I was asked to go in to see the principal. He told me that he arranged a university place in Edinburg, Scotland, with a full scholarship. But, I had to take an English exam before with a rest of the Hungarian students who were in Edinburgh, then if I passed, there was a placement to study Forestry. The scholarship was about the same as I make in the factory and my books and fees were also paid. So, 10 month after leaving Hungary, I was attending University of my choice; this was really interesting. I passed the English exam and my University fellowship was secured. I felt that I was on top of the world.

I spent 4 years at the Edinburgh University. The studying was tough but I managed all the exams and I graduated in June 1961.

I graduated in 1961 with a B.Sc. degree.

At that time, jobs were difficult to find so I looked for positions outside Britain. I was successful with the Department of Technical Cooperation and was posted to British Guiana. I spent a 3-year contract there during the turbulent years when the country was fighting for independence.

My son Michael and I in the botanical gardens in Georgetown, B.G.

My job was to lead expeditions each year to the jungle, lasting 3 months at a time. I was the only European in the expedition and I enjoyed the job very much. After 3 years, I immigrated to Canada. My first job was with the Inventory Division of the Department of Land and Forestry in Toronto. I worked as a party chief to survey the forests. After 2 years, I got another job with the Canadian Forestry Department as a Forestry Officer. In 1966-67, I went to the University of Toronto to do a Master's Degree. I specialized in Biometrics and graduated in 1967. After graduation, I got a job in Sault Ste Marie, Ontario at the Great Lakes Forest Research Centre. I was the lead scientific research for forest fertilizer projects. It was a lot of field work and I enjoyed it very much. A large part of the work was writing papers for journals and other publications.

In 1974, I received a promotion to the Pacific Research Centre in Victoria, B.C. as a Research Scientist and Senior Mensurationists. (Branch of Biometrics). I was leading mensuration research and publishing papers in journals. In 1979 I was granted another job as a Research Officer at the Inventory Branch of the Ministry of Forest in Victoria, B.C. I had the responsibility of revising the inventory practices to a modern one and introducing Geographic Information

Systems (GIS) into operation. In 1980 I was appointed Director of the Inventory Branch and continued to upgrade the modernization of forest inventory operations. I was an invited speaker at international conferences, lecturing on the upgrade of forest inventory practices and GIS. In 1990, I resigned as Director of the Branch and started my first private company, Ferihill Technologies Inc. In 1993, I established Hegyi GeoTechnologies International Inc. becoming Hegyi Geomatics International Inc. in 2000. I did a lot of business in Canada, the U.S.A. Hungary, Austria, Russia, China, Brazil, Argentina, Honduras and Chile. I stayed in the best hotels and did a lot of sightseeing. In 2016, I retired from work and am now concentrating on writing books.

Publications and Social Work

I succeeded in rebuilding my life. Now I faced another challenge: to get into scientific publications.

My first publication was my master's thesis as the Basic Density Calibration in Jack Pine stands (Hegyi 1969). I released it in the traditional manner as a journal publication.

After graduation, I was transferred to the Great Lakes Forest Research Centre (GLFRC) in Sault Ste. Marie and my first scientific publication was: Periodic Mean Annual Increment and the Derivative in Growth Prediction (Hegyi 1969). This publication was about forestry and the mathematical equations used to calculate the derivative in growth prediction. Because of my master's degree involving computers, I was inclined to continue in the field. So, at the GLFRC I was involved in the running of The Statistics and Computer Centre.

My next forays into publishing were in the relatively new self-publishing. They were aimed at research scientists who were interested in computer programming. Introduction to Programming an IBM 360/25 in Basic FORTRAN IV (Hegyi 1971) was published as an Information Report.

I also wrote an article on my thesis and other relevant forestry publications with some statistical background. Dry Matter Distribution in Jack Pine stands in Northern Ontario (Hegyi 1972) was published as an article in the Forestry Chronicle.

In 1973 I published another paper, Optimum Plot Dimensions for Experimental Designs in Jack Pine Stands (Hegyi 1973), as an information report. A year later, Planning of Experiments and Our Biases (Hegyi 1974) was released as a proceeding of the applied statistic workshop.

I published on my research work in silvicultural systems as a result of fertilizer additions as well. Testing Silvicultural Treatments by Computer Simulation (Hegyi and Tucker 1974) and What We Found: Growth

Response Evaluation of Fertilizer Trials in Jack Pine - Dryden Field Trials (Hegyi 1974) followed the Conifer Fertilization Workshop in Sault Ste. Marie.

In 1974 I was transferred from the GLFRC to Victoria and worked in the Pacific Forest Research Centre. It was a promotion from research forester to research scientist. I was involved in computer simulation modelling and had my own terminal as we were connected to IBM in Vancouver through the Cambridge Monitor System.

I published A Simulation Model for Managing Jack Pine Stands (Hegyi 1974). I also published other papers. Forest Stand Modeling Experience in Canada: An Overview for the Management Forester (Hegyi 1974) and Computer Simulation Helps manage Our Forests (Hegyi 1974) in the journal, Canadian Data Systems.

This was a period defined by state of the art technology, mimicking the growth and development of trees and stands. The computer language was FORTRAN IV and we used graphic packages to illustrate how the models were performing. I also applied the simulation modelling to growth and yield research. Growth Modelling in an Operational Planning Context (Hegyi 1975) was published as a result of the Workshop on Canadian Forest Inventory Methods, Canadian Institute of Forestry. I co-authored another article: Data Base Requirements for Growth Models in the Computer Assisted Resource Planning System in British Columbia (Glew et al 1976) which was published for the IUFRO World Congress in Norway.

Technology was changing rapidly during this period. The lab I worked in had a computer system and I was also able to communicate with the computer in Vancouver through an IBM terminal and a telephone line. At the same time, publishing technology was a changing to include the concept of self-publishing. On the research side, publications were through the Information Systems, with usually a graduate in English language as the publisher. This development was in competition with the Journal publication option. Even novel writers were getting involved in self-publishing. Usually the publisher charged the author for the cost of printing and editorial work. At the beginning, some authors were charged approximately $10,000 for the service and in return, they had a basement full of books that they had to sell. As technology developed, traditional publishing agencies were getting involved in self-publishing and they offered more reasonable options for getting books printed in lower quantities. Generally, authors promoted the sales of their book and ended up selling approximately 500 copies.

In 1979 I joined the B.C. Forest Service as a Research and Development Officer, and 1980 I was appointed Director of the Forest Inventory Program. It was a great move for my career in terms of technological enhancements. I was responsible for the re-design of the forest inventory practices, automation and Geographic Information Systems. I presented papers at international conferences as an innovator to the new technology. Automation Improves Methods of Forest Management and Inventory (Hegyi 1979) was written for the Proceedings of the International Symposium on Cartography and Computing. This article dealt with the automation processes in forest inventory when computers were introduced. The old inventory system used punch cards that had to be transferred into terminals to access the database.

In 1980 I was also published another article on the introduction of satellite based remote sensing into the forest inventory process. Overview of Forest and Range Inventory in British Columbia (Hegyi 1980) was published.

In 1981 and 1982 we published two more papers on the redesign of forest inventory Forest Classification System Considerations (Hegyi and Quenet 1981) in In-Place Resource Inventories: Principles and Practices, Proceedings of a National Workshop, Society of American Foresters, University of Maine; and Updating the Forest Inventory Data Base in British Columbia (Hegyi and Quenet 1982) in Remote Sensing for Resource Management.

In 1983 I teamed up with Dr. Pam Sallaway to solve the problem of an important aspect of overlays in graphic databases. This resulted in: Integration of Vector and Grid Data Bases in B.C. Forest Inventory (Hegyi and Sallaway 1983). It was published as a proceeding of the

Sixth International Symposium on Automated Cartography.

At this time, I also served on the National Forest Resources Inventory Committee.

As a member of the National Forest Resources Inventory Committee in 1983.

In terms of publication, I had the following papers: Integration of Remote Sensing and Computer Assisted Mapping Technology in Forestry (Hegyi and Quenet 1983) published in the Canadian Journal of Remote Sensing; Mapping and Satellite Image Analysis for Forest Inventory (Hegyi 1983) in Proceedings, Renewable Resource Inventories for Monitoring Changes and Trends, Oregon State University; Key Factors in an Operational GIS for Land Use Planning

(Hegyi 1988) in Report of a Workshop on GIS: Geographic Information Systems; The Role of GIS in Provincial Inventories (Hegyi 1989) In Proceedings, GIS 89: A Wider Perspective, Vancouver; and Possibilities and Problems in Organizing an Inventory and Monitoring Project in the Conditions of Developing Countries (Hegyi 1989), in Global Natural Resource Monitoring and Assessments.

Following that I published other articles: Remote Sensing and GIS Applications to Resource Inventory in Canada (Hegyi and Walker 1990) presented at the International Symposium on Primary Data Acquisition, Manaus, Brazil; Canada's Forest Capital. Presented at the Canada's Timber Resources (Hegyi 1990) presented at the Canada's Timber Resources – a National Conference. Victoria, B.C.; GIS, Remote Sensing and Video Technology Integration (Hegyi 1990) presented at the International Society for Photogrammetry and Remote Sensing, Commission VII, Mid-term Symposium, Victoria, British Columbia; and Multi-Resource Inventory Techniques with Remote Sensing and Geographic Information Systems (Hegyi

1990). This was presented at the International Society for Photogrammetry and Remote Sensing, Commission VII, Mid-term Symposium, Victoria, British Columbia.

In March 1990 I resigned from the government and started a private company with Penny Walker. The digitization of 7200 maps was complete and it was time to start a new venture in the private sector.

My Social Life

My marriage failed. But, I had the two precious thing: my two children in my custody

In 1969 my marriage started to fail. I was involved with the Master's thesis and computers but my wife was getting restless. She was working at the time and fell in love with her boss. He wanted her but not the children, so I was able to negotiate a divorce and keep the children in my custody. It was a very tough time for me. I was accepted to a Ph.D. program in British Columbia but with the family in turmoil, I saw my boss, Mr. Smithers, and rejected the doctoral work. I would stay with my two children, my son was 9 (Michael) and my daughter (Jennifer) 3 year old. I was making $9,000 per year and the divorce cost me $2,000. The Children's Aid Society visited me weekly. They checked that the house was clean and the children were cared for. I used to get up at 5 am and vacuum the house and tidy up. A few months later my parents came from Hungary and after one visit, the Children's Aid representative never came back.

Two years before my divorce, at Christmas time.

My wife left me in early 1969. I was looking after the two children on my own for 7 months. I met Rose McKinnon around October and we started to date with the children (my two and Rose had an 8 year old son). On June 30th, 1970 we were married.

In 1970 we married with the children participating.

Our wedding cake.

The picture shows my wife, mother and daughter, Jennifer.

My family with my parents in Victoria, B.C. in 1980

In addition to publication, I was involved in social work while I lived in Victoria. In particular, I was President of the Oak Bay Minor Hockey Association, funding chair of Oldtimers Hockey Tournament, and governor of Kiwanis International.

My time as President of the Oak Bay Minor Hockey (Centre).

As Minor Hockey president, we hosted the 2nd Annual Old Timers Tournament. Our guest: Cyclone Taylor.

I was elected as Governor of the Pacific North West Kiwanis Organization in 1990

I was honored by the Kiwanis Club of Ottawa for 35 years of service.

In Kyoto, Japan 1988, with the ISPRS (International Society of Photogrammetry and Remote Sensing) getting elected to President VII. (GIS). Next to me is Dr. Goodenough of the Government of Canada

As a member of a delegation to the Soviet Union in 1982. This meeting is with Dr. Moroz (Head of Inventory of All Union Forests) in Moscow.

Meeting with our host in St Petersburg. The host (far right) was a famous referee of hockey.

In 1983 I visited China and gave a presentation on space age computer techniques.

Advising the United Commercial Travelers on computer systems in Columbus, Ohio, 1987

My wife Rose and I, enjoying life.

Joining the Private Sector

After 23 years in government, I decided to join the private sector as President of my company. I held this job for 25 years

I started a computer science company in 1990, focusing on wireless data transmission, global positioning acquisition and tracking of vehicles.

At first (1990-93), as Ferihill Technologies Ltd., we were involved in a variety of new projects:

1. Industrial Research Assistance Program (IRAP) help us to develop an Airborne Digital Imaging System (ADD/IS).

The focus of this project was the automation of aerial photo interpretation systems for digital processing. These systems were then installed at the Pacific Forestry Research Centre in Victoria, B.C., and at Aerodata, in Brazil.

2. A second project was the development of the Ferihill Imaging System for Correction (FISC).

This project was based in the development of ADD/IS for applications in digital image processing. We installed an image capture board into a personal computer and processed images of people and identification systems. Fourteen stations were installed across Canada.

3. The Ferihill Asset Management Information System (FAMIS).

This product was developed from (ADD/IS) in the B.C Ministry of Forests and Purchasing Commission. It was used for the assets of the Ministry's management system. We catalogued each product in the warehouse, including images and descriptions, and set up an image retrieval system for the inventory.

4. Review of the Forest Resources Inventory program, a contract with the Ontario Ministry of Natural Resources.

The Forest Resources Inventory system has been in place since the late 1940's. It provided provincial coverage which was summarized and published in 1963. There have been modifications to this system since its inception, although the overall basic design is still that of the 1940's and 1950's. Forest management practices have, however, changed significantly during the last decade and the information required for these changes resulted in a review of the FRI production processes and products.

Over 140 people were interviewed as part of the review process. In addition, the evaluation team examined, in detail, the various aspects of the FRI process. They reviewed relevant literature and resource inventory practices in other jurisdictions. The report contains the results of the FRI review, including recommendations for major changes in both the FRI methodology and the existing infrastructure. A report entitled "Review of the Ontario Inventories Program" was prepared and presented to a review committee.

We also published the following papers: Multi-Resource Inventories with Air and Space Borne Digital Remote Sensing (Hegyi and Walker 1991), Tomorrow's

Vision, a Reality Today. GIS 91, Vancouver, B.C.; Replacing Aerial Photo Interpretation in Resource Inventories with Integrated Digital Images and GIS (Hegyi at all 1992) in GIS 92, Vancouver, B.C.; ISPRS Congress: Replacing Aerial Photos in Resource Inventories with Airborne Digital Data and GIS (Hegyi et al. 1992) in XVII Congress of the ISPRS, Washington, D.C.; and Multi-resource Inventories with Remote Sensing, GIS and Video Imaging (Hegyi 1992) in the 6th Australasian Remote Sensing Conference, Wellington, New Zealand.

In 1993, Penny Walker and I decided to develop a separate company. I formed Hegyi GeoTechnologies International Inc. I focused on forestry applications in the international business sector. A summary of the projects that we implemented are:

1. Re-Engineering the Forest Resources Inventory System.

A priority in the Ministry of Natural Resources' strategic direction is to enhance the information and knowledge base that supports resource management in

Ontario. Natural resource inventories are fundamental to effective resource management. Under this direction, as part of a corporately sanctioned strategic planning process, the Ministry commissioned a consortium to review the Forest Resource Inventory Program. A report entitled: A Review of the Ontario Forest Resources Inventory Program was presented to the Ministry in 1993.

As the next step in the development of a strategic plan, the Natural Resources Inventories Section hosted a Strategic Planning Workshop with a broad cross section of users, targeted towards the re-engineering of the FRI. This report contains the proceedings of this workshop.

This was a joint venture project with the Technical and Administrative Branch of the British Columbia Ministry of Forest and Geomatics Canada of the Canadian Forest Service. It studied a Mobile Communications Centre (MCC) for forest management and environmental monitoring. A primary purpose of this development is to facilitate the digital data through the use of telecommunication technology, including the repositioning of vehicle based mobile units through the use of wireless data from Global Positioning system (GPS) satellites. This report includes a review of potential MCC hardware technology including: research and support information on hardware requirements for MCC units; information and recommendations on the most suitable candidate equipment for MCC units; and review of destructive and non-destructive tests of candidate equipment. The report also included the evaluation of technologies and reports on the minimum requirements for other MCC hardware components, including: MCC unit mounting platform and support structure, location in a vehicle and interface connections; interfaces of MCC units to optional devices; and power source, and power distribution options. The report concludes with an evaluation of the minimum hardware requirements for the Base Station Communications Centre (BSCC) and discusses BSCC access and interface requirements to Local Area Networks LAN(s) and other external systems such as on-line bulletin board systems (BBS) for real-time differential GPS correction.

4. British Columbia Ferries Corporation Ship-to-Shore Wireless Communication Pilot Project

The British Columbia Ferry Corporation (BCFC) manages one of the largest and most advanced ferry fleets in the world. The Corporation is currently in the process of implementing a ten-year plan to ensure that the provincial ferry system can meet anticipated growth patterns well into the next century. The examination of emerging communications technologies is a critical part of the planning process, particularly the use of ship-to-shore wireless data transmission. This has the capability to provide significant benefits to the corporation in a variety of application areas. The goal of this pilot project was to evaluate existing and emerging wireless communications technologies in light of their applicability for BCFC ship-to-shore applications. They were assessed for their reliability and costs compared to conventional ship-to-shore data communications methods currently being employed by the corporation. To accomplish these extensive field tests, a range of wireless carriers and communications devices were performed onboard the MV Queen of Cowichan on the Nanaimo-Horseshoe Bay route.

In this report, the results of the analysis are presented in a matrix format that allows easy evaluation and comparison between the various wireless options.

5. GeoSmart Mobile Office.

The GeoSmart Mobile Office was designed to provide urgently needed solutions to the problem of delivering geo-referenced land information that can be queried in the field to answer user-specific questions.

Land information systems developed by Provincial and Federal Government agencies are highly sophisticated and contain relatively up-to-date information. However, these databases are generally in central locations such as headquarters, regional and district offices, and are not available in a flexible and retrievable form for resource officers and land managers who make their decisions in the field.

The GeoSmart Mobile Office presented offered a cost-effective solution to the problem with significant positive impacts on management practices that affect our environment. It offered the essential tools for collecting site specific information in the field, on-line expert consultation with specialists who were in regional or district offices, and facilitated immediate action to stop practices which were damaging to the environment. It is offering a user-friendly technology to resources and environmental managers in the field.

Hegyi GeoTechnologies International Inc. (HGI), in cooperation with the B.C. Ministry of Forests, completed a feasibility study on wireless transmission of natural resource and environmental monitoring data between mobile field units and District Offices. Consequently, Hegyi GeoTechnologies International Inc. built a conceptual prototype mobile office, with GeoSmart (Geotechnology Solutions with a Multimedia Applications Resource Tool book) technology, to prove the concept and the economic benefits of transmitting digital data between a district office and a mobile unit. Hegyi GeoTechnologies International Inc. now plans to proceed with the development of an operational GeoSmart Mobile Office, followed by the creation of a manufacturing facility. We plan to use industry standard technology in the development of the GeoSmart Mobile Office.

The objective of the proposed Mobile Office was to provide digital spatial data and other relevant information to resource and environmental managers in the field. This information included location capabilities with a Global Positional System (GPS), wireless digital data transmission, logistical decision support and voice command interface, stereo viewing of aerial photos, and direct interface with GIS. The interface would allow for the acquisition of digital data, and computer visualization of the impacts of resource management practices on the environment.

6. GIS Applications with pen-based hand held computers.

This project, under the Geographic Information System Development Program (GISDP), focused on exploring ways to promote the use and marketing of the spatial information data of Geomatics Canada through HGI's Mobile Technical Office (MTO). In particular, the objective was to capitalize on the investment of HGI in the development and marketing of MTO (over $3 million) by incorporating Geomatics Canada's spatial information in future sales of the product. It was recognized, at the start, that the marketing of MTO with Geomatics Canada's digitized maps could be made more successful through the use of hand-held pen-based computers as delivery tools. Hence, the initial focus of the project was to enhance MTO capabilities, which were restricted to vehicle-based operations. It would enhance field conditions by developing a prototype system that fit into a pack sack and used a hand-held pen-based computer integrated with GPS and wireless communication capabilities. The research and development that was necessary for the development of such a prototype was also supported through financial contributions from NRC.

I visited Hungary in 2000. My nephew, sister, daughter and another nephew in our village.

We tranferred the technology to Guatemala in 2001.

Addressing the Kiwanis Club of Ottawa on technological development in 2001.

Gave a demonstration of the Mobile Office to the Canadian Ambassador (left in front) in Budapest in 2002.

Visited India 14 times, demonstrating the advantages of wireless data transmission and emergency preparedness.

I was member of the scientific delegation to India, led by the Canadian Minister of International Trade (4th from the right)

Staff golf tournament in Ottawa in 2003

In India playing golf with Asok Mookerjee (left) in 2004

In Russia with my former Deputy Minister of Forestry, Mike Apsey (second on left), a Deputy Minister of Forests in Russia, and Dr. Maleshiva who was working with me.

I am active with the Circle K Club (sponsored by the Ottawa Kiwanis Club). In this picture, the International President of Kiwanis presents the Membership to the local Circle K President.

My mother visiting us in Canada in 2004 (her 8th visit).

We also published the following papers: Remote Sensing and Geographic Information Systems (GIS) Applications for Multi-Resource Inventories in Canada (Hegyi 1995) in The Canadian Remote Sensing Contribution to Understanding Global Change. Edited by E. LeDrew, M. Strome and F. Hegyi. Department of Geography Publications Series, No. 38; Challenges in Wireless Data Transmission. In Proceedings of Canada Disaster Management Workshop (Hegyi 1993) in Proceedings of Canada Disaster Management Workshop, held in Ottawa, Canada; and GIS and GPS based asset management for Road and Railway Transportation Systems in India (Hegyi and Mookerjee 1993) Proceedings of Map India 2003, published on a Conference website.

During this period, I was travelling around the world promoting the new technology. I had projects in Hungary, Russia, China, Brazil, Argentina and the United States and demonstrated its advantages. But at the same time, I was planning to write a novel of my adventures in life and particularly, my travels in different cultures.

Traditional Publications of Books

In 2004 my passion for writing books resurfaced. I was facing another challenge: to become an author of my books. I decided to write about my travels around the world. Since I was unfamiliar with novel promotion, I decided to pursue traditional publication.

The customary methods of book publication was changing during this period. "A traditional book publishing company buys the rights to an author's manuscript. Usually an agent, representing the author, negotiates the deal with the book publisher and in return gets a percentage of any monies earned from the sale of the author's book. Part of the arrangement includes payment of an advance by the book publisher to the author to secure the book deal. In return, the author, working with an in-house editor, is expected to finish writing the book in an allotted time - which is often years away. The advance is deducted by the book publisher from any royalties the author receives from the sale of the book. Royalties are based on a mutually agreed upon percentage of sales. The author does not receive any royalties until the advance is paid back in full. The book publisher budgets funds to promote and market the book - this amount varies greatly depending on the marketability of the book. The author is often strongly encouraged to hire a book publicist and to work aggressively to promote their book. The book publisher has the final say on every aspect of the author's book, from editorial content to cover design to the number of books in the first printing. The book publisher makes the determination, based on declining sales, as to when to allow a book to go out of print - this could be as short as a year or even less. Authors beware - some traditional publishing houses are putting their out of stock or back-list titles into commercial print on demand systems so the book isn't technically out of print and the book's rights will never revert back to the author"[3].

If you are new to the publishing world and unaware of what a literary agent does, the above quoted

---

[3] http://www.infinitypublishing.com/book-publishing-faqs/what-is-traditional-book-publishing.html

article should be of some help to you. Literary agents take your manuscript and present it to publishers in an attempt to garner a contract with a publishing company. If an agent manages this, they will negotiate the terms of the publication contract on your behalf. They usually earn a commission from each sale of your book. Literary agents can be a useful asset to writers, but attaining one is difficult. In fact, many agents will not read manuscripts from new authors, let alone represent them. In my opinion it's harder to get a literary agent to represent you than it is to get a publisher to publish you[4].

When I completed my first book "Dare to Survive," I explored the publication media. This book covers my global travel, introduction to different cultures, political systems and peoples.

A brief synopsis of the book: This is a collection of heart-warming stories of survival, illustrated with humorous anecdotes. The stories include:

- Surviving World War II and its aftermath in Europe. It includes Nazi and Soviet occupations

---

[4] http://www.2publishabook.com/bookpublishers.html

in Hungary and living in bunkers as the front moved through the village.
- Surviving the 1956 Hungarian Revolution as a freedom fighter and escaping to Austria 3 hours before scheduled execution.
- Re-building life as a refugee, including graduation with a B.Sc. and M.Sc. degrees.
- Surviving expeditions to the jungles and racial riots in British Guiana, South America, during the early 1960's.
- Challenges of integrating into Canadian society and climbing the professional ladder as a high tech entrepreneur.
- Returning to the old country for a visit after 18 years and seeing that the communist regime was still controlling the lives of its citizens.
- Visiting the Soviet Union in 1982 as member of a Canadian scientific delegation. As well, difficult encounters with KGB officials who knew details of my past as a former freedom fighter.

- Rising to top positions in volunteer work as an ice hockey coach/organizer and District Governor with Kiwanis International.
- Surviving life-threatening moments and economic challenges during cancer treatments.

My first strategy was to seek a literary agent. I sent individual letters to about 30 agents and when they inquired about the book, I sent the above synopsis. Some agents ask me to send them a manuscript, reviewed it, and sent back a note to say it wasn't in their realm of interest. I corresponded with a few in more detail, but we did not come to an agreement.

I approached publishers directly after that. Several companies expressed interest, but I chose a local one, Baco Publishing of Ottawa. The president of the company reviewed the book and found it interesting. He suggested changing the title to "Dare to Take the Next Step." I signed a contract with them, provided a manuscript and pictures. About 3 weeks later, the proof was ready to review. The final book design:

This publication sold approximately 500 copies, an average performance by an author who has not sold any books previously.

I published another book with Baco, "Death Can Wait: Stories from Cancer Survivors." The authors were:

Frank Hegyi is a scientist, entrepreneur and author. He has spent over 38 years in community service. He is a past District Governor of Kiwanis International. At age 66, he was diagnosed with prostate cancer. During radiation treatment, he wrote a book about his life experiences entitled: <u>Dare to Take the Next Step.</u>

Roslyn Franken, diagnosed with cancer at age 29, fought back to become a long-term survivor. Roslyn now provides Motivational Speaking and Personal Counseling services using the principles she developed. They are shared in her book: <u>The A List: 9 Guiding Principles for Healthy Eating and Positive Living</u>.

Jacquelin Holzman is a former mayor of Ottawa (1991–1997), with more than 15 years' experience in politics and over 50 years of community service. A few months after leaving the mayor's office, she was diagnosed with breast cancer. It was treated successfully and she became an advocate for breast cancer related causes. Jackie and her daughter have raised over $200,000 for cancer care and

research at The Ottawa Hospital and the Ottawa Health Research Institute during the past 10 years.

Max Keeping is VP of News at CTV Ottawa, and anchor of its flagship 6pm newscast for 36 years. His community involvement has helped raise more than $100 million charitable dollars. He's received the Order of Canada, Order of Ontario, a Gemini Humanitarian Award, and an honorary degree from the University of Ottawa. A wing of the Children's Hospital (CHEO) is named in his honour. He survived prostate cancer, but another form took him away in October of 2015.

This was a popular book, released on the event of "Dancing in the Street", which was organized by Max Keeping. The cover of the publication is:

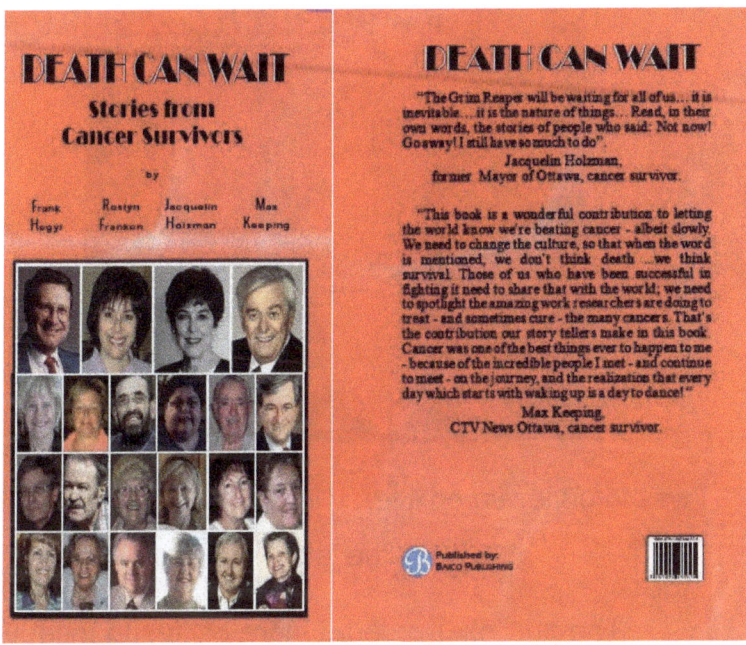

This form of book sold about 800 copies. It was promoted by television and sold in the local book stores. The proceeds were all donated to the Ottawa Cancer Foundation.

I was interviewed on live TV with Jaquelin Holzman (on the left).

The publisher ordered more copies to meet book store demand. However, the local market was saturated and the books returned to the publisher. I bought over 800 copies from the publisher in returned sales.

With technological changes, and especially the popular acceptance of eBooks, traditional publishers are switching to a self-publishing style of communication. This is influence by the fact that each year in North America over 1 million publications occur, mostly in self-publishing. Added to this development, the spread of blog publishing is becoming increasingly popular. I decided to explore self-publishing options for my next book.

Self-publishing of Books

Traditional publications are for the famous and accomplished authors. Self-publishing for the rest of us.

Several publishing companies were promoting self-publishing as an alternative. Lists of self-publishing companies are available on the internet. I settled on Lightning Source by Ingram and am satisfied with the service.

Lightning Source by Ingram

LIGHTNING® print on demand & distribution services. U.S. or U.K. publishers who desire to expand their borders can do so easily with Lightning Source. They make it easy to reach international markets and distribute books effectively, without expensive and unwieldy transatlantic shipping. For example: "We deliver solutions that enable UK titles reach US readers,

Spanish publishers reach the Spanish speaking population in the U.S.[5]"

Lightning Source gives the publishing community options to print books in any quantity, and provides its customers access to the most comprehensive bookselling channel in the industry. The average cost of books is $5 per copy.

My transition was very smooth. The books are printed in a word document and converted to a .pdf format (with some specifications) and the process is complete.

If you are not comfortable with publishing guidelines, hire a computer science graduate and he/she will work with the publisher. The average cost of printed copy will be reduced from about $10 to approximately $5 a copy. Then you can choose the selling price (ex. $15 per copy). It can be set for on-demand publication.

In this process, the author is responsible for the promotion of the book and the Internet has many

---

[5] https://www.lightningsource.com/

suggestions for promoting agencies. Research this question quite a bit because you can lose some money if you choose an inexperienced or unconnected promoter.

Lightning source is a good international company and books are made available through Amazon among other online book sellers. To look at my books on www.amazon.com, type in 'Frank Hegyi.' A list of my publications is given and you can purchase online.

My web site

I have also purchased a professional web site, www.hegyipublication.com

Home screen

Welcome to my page: www.hegyipublication.com .

Web hosting: frankhegyi.blogspot.ca

Journey to the Big World

Visit www.amazon.com type in Frank Hegyi.

Visit frankhegyi.bolgspot.ca

Read about my journeys around the world

The Thee Revolutionaries

Demonstrating GIS technology to forester in 1980

The Stroke

Visit www.amazoon.com type in Frank Hegyi.

Visit frankhegyi.blogspot.ca

On February 19th 2011 I was at home waiting for my daughter to come over for breakfast. It was the day before my grandson's 8th birthday: after breakfast we were planning to shop around for his birthday present. During breakfast, my daughter observed me looking at the paper aggressively. When she asked me what was the matter, I did not respond and only vacantly stared. My daughter Jennifer hurried to give me support as I was gradually phasing out of consciousness. My wife, Rose, helped Jennifer escort me to the car. **I was suffering from a stroke.**

Within a week, a doctor told my wife that she should get used to my "vegetative" existence. It was going to be a permanent fixture if I survived. It was a severe stroke and the chances were that I would be partially paralyzed. During the second week, my family was told that it was doubtful that I would even survive. My condition was worsening and doctors induced a coma. I was in that state for a week before they nursed me back to an unconscious state.

For the next 4 weeks in hospital, recovery was tough. I could see the family around me talking, visiting me daily, but I could not talk to them. The grandchildren visited me but were not aware of my struggle to survive. Apart from my leg and arms which seemed paralyzed, movements were limited. The tubes that I had in my mouth annoyed me and I tried to take them out. But the nurses kept them in place so I could get oxygen as I recovered from my paralysis.

After about 4 weeks, I opened my eyes and I saw Rose holding my hand. I managed to say "Hi." Rose was very excited by this communication. She called over the nurse and they talked to me. I vaguely understood what they were saying and I tried to say a few words. My limited vocabulary was about 20 words, but I could communicate.

When I was alone in bed, I visualized walking again. I started to get my legs into motion, then my arms, to get them into practice. It was hard but I had hope that I would walk again. I practiced for about half an hour each day and movement started to return. The arm was going to require more practice and the leg wanted a little more time.

This book tells the struggles of walking again, re-learning language, and recovering from partial paralysis.

By Christmas I visited my son in Madison, WI without a cane.

Death Can Wait

Visit www.amazon.com and type in Frank Hegyi

Visit frankhegyi.blogspot.ca

The quartet who put together this book, Frank Hegyi, Roslyn Franken, Jacquelin Holzman, and Max Keeping, all share a trait in common - the desire, and ability, to transcend their own personal circumstances and help others.

They have battled cancer, and as soldiers in this struggle, they have come together to offer help of a most vital sort. Facts and details about cancer in its many forms are readily available. What is not as easy to find is true, unvarnished insight into what goes on behind the scenes, behind the outer facade.

What goes through peoples' minds when they get the shattering news? What feelings and emotions do they wrestle with, as they cling onto life? Which attitudes are helpful or destructive?

This book addresses these issues. Each contributor has their own unique story, one they give to the world. It takes courage and precision to be able to share, to reveal what really goes on. We are so grateful to those who have given in this profound manner.

This is so important for those who unfortunately are destined to be told they have cancer, a steadily rising number of between one-third and one-half of the population. No two cancers or two individuals are alike. But we all share a common desire to live, to be healthy, and to have the necessary wherewithal to surmount life-threatening crises.

This book provides so much of that in a personal, even intimate way. The battle against cancer is being fought on so many fronts - research, treatment, prevention, etc. The emotional side cannot be ignored. This is a book about feelings in times of gigantic challenge. May it enable others to feel better a little bit. Five of the contributors, including Max Keeping, have passed away.

Authors Frank Hegyi, Roslyn Franken and Jackie Holzman sell <u>Death Can Wait</u> at the Dancing on the Street promotion.

If It Wasn't for Celibacy... I Would Have Been a Priest

Visit www.amazon.com type in Frank Hegyi. Visit frankhegyi.blogspot.ca

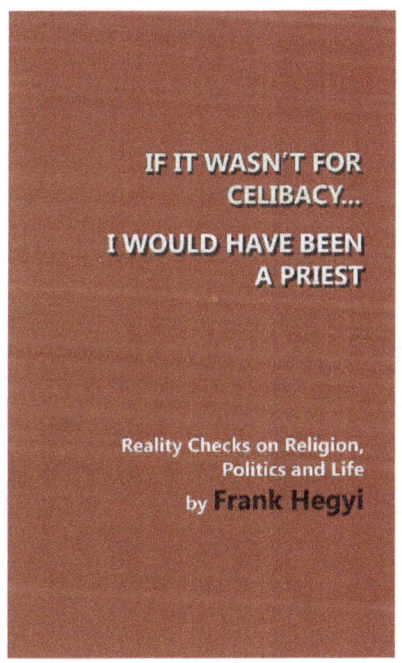

Renowned author Frank Hegyi offers a lighthearted insight on current events of religion, politics and life. His world travels have given him a unique perspective on present and historical events. From living in communism, escaping a country in conflict and leading a full career in the public service and private sector, he writes on the subjects that touch him the most. Sit back, relax and enjoy his unique viewpoints on the topics that are at the forefront of news today.

Social Media Promotions

I found success in self-publishing through the Social Media. I have written 5 books and marketing is increasingly good.

Promotion of novels may be accomplished through social media tools. Social media has been broadly defined as many relatively inexpensive and widely accessible electronic tools that enable anyone to publish and access information, collaborate on a common effort, or build relationships. Social media technologies take on many different forms, including blogs, business networks, enterprise social networks, forums, microblogs, photo sharing, products/services review, social bookmarking, social gaming, social networks, video sharing and virtual worlds. The top social media questions marketers want answered can be summarized as: tactics, engagement, measurement, audience and tools. As the social media marketing industry continues to expand and change, the needs of marketers are clear[6].

Social media marketing is still growing. For businesses, social media is essential, as you'll see detailed in this year's report. More than 3700 marketers surveyed provided the kind of insight you won't find elsewhere.

Tools for social media marketing are numerous, but there is an associated coast. A partial list follows:

---

[6] Social Media Marketing Industry Report

Facebook

Facebook is an online social networking service headquartered in Menlo Park, California. Its website was launched on February 4, 2004, by Mark Zuckerberg and associates. The founders had initially limited the website's membership to Harvard students, but later expanded it to colleges in the Boston area. It gradually added support for students at various other universities and later to high-school students. Since 2006, everyone is allowed to become a registered user of the website, though the age requirement may be higher depending on applicable local laws

After registering to use the site, users can create a user profile, add other users as "friends", exchange messages, post status updates and photos, share videos and receive notifications when others update their profiles. Additionally, users may join common-interest user groups. Facebook, Inc. held its initial public offering in February 2012 and began selling stock to the public three months later, reaching an original peak market capitalization of $104 billion. On July 13, 2015,

Facebook became the fastest company in the Standard & Poor's 500 Index to reach a market cap of $250 billion.

The Book Promoters

I have chosen The Book Promoters to publicize my books. They advertise in the following media:
- Major Search Engine Placement
- Kindle Book Tour Blogs
- National Press Releases
- Book Traffic
- Facebook Advertisements
- Store Link Advertisements
- Book Blogger Advertisements
- Blog Bomb (for bloggers)

Publishing a book has opened many doors for me but all authors realize it's not easy to sell their book. The Book Promoters have successfully accomplished marketing books for over 9 years through direct online channels and release targeting. They started as a marketing company for small businesses. Later, they took on the challenge of finding the line between successes with a publisher and obtaining the same without one. Major publishers handle the book, selling and marketing but with self-publishing, that remains the responsibility of the author. Many self-published books are digital, requiring a source for digital marketing. The Book Promoters use search engine placement for all major programs, apps for your books if needed, book blog promotion so bloggers can tell their readers about you, ad marketing advertisement on mobile devices, social networks, news, book channels and more. They are considered a "one stop" as book authors need an army not just to sell books, but also to beat the competition. To see more, consult www.thebookpromoter.com

I am using the book promoters for the marketing of my five books:

1. Journey to the Big World.
2. The Stroke.
3. Death Can Wait
4. If It Wasn't for Celibacy... I Would Have Been a Priest.
5. The Three Revolutionaries.

Epilogue

I dedicate this book to my Grandfather and my Mother.

My family was involved in a series of revolutions. My great-great Grandfather, a nobleman, was actively involved in politics, and joined the 1848 revolution against the Hapsburg Empire. They were victorious in Buda against the Croatian forces, but he lost his life in Világos (now Şiria, Romania) in 1849. He was buried with the poet Petőfi in a mass grave after the battle. He was a true patriot of Hungary and sacrificed his life for the country.

My grandfather tried to rebuild the estate. He bought land in Nyőgér and was a successful farmer. He became a notary public servant and he and his wife commissioned a statue in the church yard to commemorate his good fortunes. I had a special relationship with Grandfather.

In 1948 his youngest son, István was sentenced for death after he crossed the border to Yougslavia. It was a crime on the orders of Rákosi (the prime Minister), for being the friend of Marshall Tito. He spent 5 years in a death camp and was told, after he got too weak to work, you can die out of starvation. Some of the torture methods were designed by Rákosi himself. After 5 years, István was freed when Imre Nagy became the Prime Minister.

I took part in the revolution in 1956 and after its defeat, I managed to escape 3 hours before I was scheduled to be shot. On the way to the border, I was recaptured by Russian soldiers but managed to escape. I rebuilt my life in the west, having graduated with a B.Sc. and M.Sc degrees. I remained a research scientist for 10 years, then a Director in Government (for another 10), and after that I ran a private company for 25 years. Then I started to write books. I was the lucky one!

I dedicate this book to my grandfather, Mihály Hegyi, who was a great influence on my career, and my mother, Piri Sarolta, who stood by me in difficult times. She helped me to go to high school, even though my father objected to it. She visited me in Canada 8 times and was proud of my achievements.

I am the author of 36 publications in Journals and Proceedings and have written 4 books. The 5th is now being published: **The Three Revolutionaries.** This book is my story about the revolutions my great-great grandfather, my Uncle István and I got involved in the 1956.

I have had a healthy life, only interrupted by cancer in 2004 and a stroke in 2011. I have recovered from both illnesses, and am healthy at age 78.

I thank you, God, for looking after me!

Literature Cited

Hegyi, F., 1969. *A Study of Basic Density Variation in Jack Pine.* M.Sc.F. Thesis, University of Toronto. 85p.

Hegyi, F., 1969. *Periodic Mean Annual Increment and the Derivative in Growth Prediction.* Forest Res. Lab., Sault Ste. Marie. Information Report O-X-140. 36p.

Hegyi, F., 1971. *Introduction to Programming an IBM 360/25 in "Basic FORTRAN IV" Language.* Forest Res. Lab., Sault Ste. Marie. Information Report O-X-152. 49p.

Hegyi, F., 1972. *Dry Matter Distribution in Jack Pine stands in Northern Ontario.* Forestry Chronicle 48(4): pp 193-197.

Hegyi, F., 1973. *Optimum Plot Dimensions for Experimental Designs in jack Pine Stands.* Forest Res. Lab., Sault Ste. Marie. Information Report O-X-181. 15p.

Hegyi, F., 1974. *Planning of Experiments and Our Biases.* Proc. Applied Statistics Workshop, Environment Canada, Ottawa. 4p.

Hegyi, F. and Tucker, T.L., 1974. *Testing Silvicultural Treatments by Computer Simulation.* Proc. Conifer Fertilization Workshop, Sault Ste. Marie. Canadian Forestry

Hegyi, F., 1974. *What We Found: Growth Response Evaluation of Fertilizer Trials in Jack Pine - Dryden Field Trials.* Proc. Conifer Fertilization Workshop, Sault Ste. Marie.

Hegyi, F., 1974. *A Simulation Model for Managing Jack Pine Stands.* In Growth Models for Tree and Stand Simulation. Proc. Int. Union Forest Res. Org., Vancouver, 1973. Edited by J. Fries. pp 74-90.

Hegyi, F., 1974. *Forest Stand Modeling Experience in Canada: An Overview for the Management Forester.* Proc. Joint Workshop of

Midwest Forest Mensurationists and Biometricians, School of Natural Resources, University of Wisconsin. pp15-19.

Hegyi, F., 1974. Computer Simulation Helps manage Our Forests. Canadian Data Systems 6:33.

Hegyi, F., 1975. Growth Modeling in an Operational Planning Context. Proc. Workshop on Canadian Forest Inventory Methods, Canadian Institute of Forestry. University of Toronto Press. pp 224-239.

Glew, D.R., Hegyi, F. and Honer, T.G., 1976. Data Base Requirements for Growth Models in the Computer Assisted Resource Planning System in British Columbia. Proc. VI IUFRO World Congress, Norway. pp 74-85.

Hegyi, F., 1979. "Automation Improves Methods of Forest Management and Inventory". In Proceedings of the International Symposium on Cartography and Computing: Applications in health and Environment. Volume I, pp 554-558

Hegyi, F., 1979. "Automation Improves Methods of Forest Management and Inventory". In Proceedings of the International Symposium on Cartography and Computing: Applications in health and Environment. Volume I, pp 554-558

Hegyi, F., 1980. Overview of forest and Range Inventory in British Columbia. In Proceedings of the Ecological Data Processing and Interpretation Workshop, Victoria, British Columbia. pp 1-16.

Hegyi, F. and Quenet, R.V., 1981. Forest Classification System Considerations. In In-Place Resource Inventories: Principles and Practices, Proceedings of a National Workshop, Society of American Foresters, University of Maine, August 9-14, 1981. Pp 69-74.

Hegyi, F. and Quenet, R.V., 1982. Updating the Forest Inventory Data Base in British Columbia. In Remote Sensing for Resource Management. Iowa: Soil conservation Society of America: Ch. 46 pp 512-518.

Hegyi, F. and Sallaway, P., 1983. Integration of Vector and Grid Data Bases in B.C. Forest Inventory. In Auto Carto Six, Proceedings of the Sixth International Symposium on Automated Cartography. Vol. I: pp 215 - 221.

Hegyi, F. and Quenet, R.V., 1983. Integration of Remote Sensing and Computer Assisted Mapping Technology in Forestry: Canadian Journal of Remote Sensing, Vol. 9(2), pp 92-98.

Hegyi, F., 1983, Mapping and Satellite Image Analysis for Forest Inventory. In Proceedings, Renewable Resource Inventories for Monitoring Changes and Trends, Oregon State University, Corvallis.

Hegyi, F., 1988. Key Factors in an Operational GIS for Land Use Planning. In Report of a Workshop on GIS: Geographic Information Systems, ESCAP/UNDP, Bangkok, Thailand.

Hegyi, F., 1989. The Role of GIS in Provincial Inventories. In Proceedings, GIS 89: A Wider Perspective, Vancouver, Canada.

Hegyi, F., 1989. Possibilities and Problems in Organizing an Inventory and Monitoring Project in the Conditions of Developing Countries, Presented at: Global Natural Resource Monitoring and Assessments: Preparing for the 21st Century, Venice, Italy.

Hegyi, F., and Walker, P.A., 1990. Remote Sensing and GIS Applications to Resource Inventory in Canada, Presented at: International Symposium on Primary Data Acquisition, Manaus, Brazil.

Hegyi, F. 1990. Canada's Forest Capital. Presented at the Canada's Timber Resources – a National Conference. Victoria, B.C.

Hegyi, F., 1990. GIS, Remote Sensing and Video Technology Integration, Presented at: International Society for Photogrammetry and Remote Sensing, Commission VII, Mid-term Symposium, Victoria, British Columbia.

Hegyi, F., 1990. Multi-Resource Inventory Techniques with Remote Sensing and Geographic Information Systems, Presented at: International Society for Photogrammetry and Remote Sensing, Commission VII, Mid-term Symposium, Victoria, British Columbia

Hegyi, F., Walker, P. 1991. Multi Resource Inventories with Air and Space Borne Digital Remote Sensing, GIS and Vide Imaging: Tomorrow's Vision, a Reality Today. GIS 91, Vancouver, B.C.

Hegyi, F., Pilon, P., Walker, P. 1992. Replacing Aerial Photo Interpretation in Resource Inventories with Integrated Digital Images and GIS. GIS 92, Vancouver, B.C.

Hegyi, F., Pilon, P., Walker, P. 1992. ISPRS Congress Replacing Aerial Photos in Resource Inventories with Airborne Digital Data and GIS. XVII Congress of the ISPRS, Washington, D.C.

Hegyi, F. 1992. Multi-resource Inventories with Remote Sensing, GIS and Video Imaging, 6th Australasian Remote Sensing Conference, Wellington, New Zealand.

Hegyi, F. 1995. Remote Sensing and Geographic Information Systems (GIS) Applications for Multi-Resource Inventories in Canada. In The Canadian Remote Sensing Contribution to Understanding Global Change. Edited by E. LeDrew, M. Strome and F. Hegyi. Department of Geography Publications Series, No. 38, University of Waterloo.

Hegyi. F. 2001. Challenges in Wireless Data Transmission. In Proceedings of Canada Disaster Management Workshop, held in Ottawa, Canada on October 22-23, 2001

Hegyi, F. and A.K Mookerjee. 2003. GIS and GPS based asset management for Road and Railway Transportation Systems in India Proceedings of Map India 2003, published in a Conference website.

http://www.gisdevelopment.net/application/utility/transport/mi03187.htm

www.ingramcontent.com/pod-product-compliance
Lightning Source LLC
Chambersburg PA
CBHW070200100426
42743CB00013B/2983